salmonpoetry

Publishing Irish & International
Poetry Since 1981

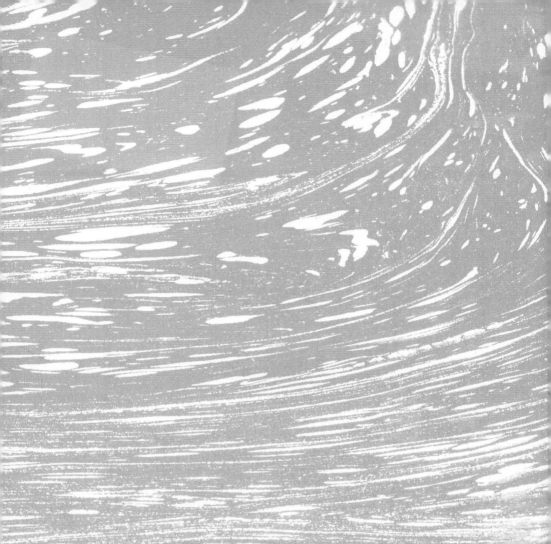

ALSO BY RUTH O'CALLAGHAN

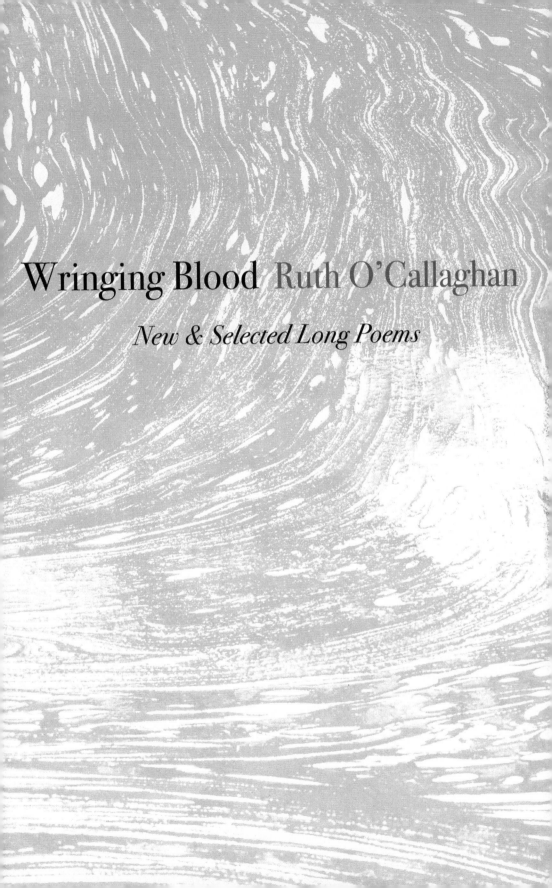

Wringing Blood Ruth O'Callaghan

New & Selected Long Poems

Published in 2018 by

Salmon Poetry

Cliffs of Moher, County Clare, Ireland

Website: www.salmonpoetry.com

Email: info@salmonpoetry.com

ISBN 978-1-912561-33-9

COVER PHOTOGRAPHY: Jessie Lendennie

COVER DESIGN & TYPESETTING: *Siobhán Hutson*

Printed in Ireland by Sprint Print

For Christine

without those love and encouragement

this book would never have happened

Contents

from

An Unfinished Sufficiency

(Salmon Poetry, 2015)

Perspective

It is February. From the tracks beyond the cemetery
the last train defies the dark, defies the dark

beyond the cemetery. It is February. Onto the tracks
a body may fall, fall from the bridge

the bridge that springs over the tracks, the tracks
on which a body may span, horizontal

east to west or west to east, never north to south
south to north. Horizontal.

Too late, too late to grind the brakes, the brakes
too late if a body breaks on the tracks.

The woman at the window sees the man on the bridge
to the man on the bridge the woman at the window cries *Wait*.

Spanning the tracks that the driver can see
but not a body spanning the tracks

there is no body spanning the tracks as he moves on,
moves on defying the dark

beyond the cemetery. It is February. The rails are sharp
the night is clear, he is on time.

The driver's on time. All is ordered in this dark. He's taken advice.
He can implement procedures. Procedures.

Vera climbs the stairs of the bridge, sees the man on the bridge
hears the cry of the woman at the window but not the word.

                                        She is alone.

He cuts a swathe towards the tunnel. He is on time
he is a man who defies the dark

he is a man moving on, moving on through the night
the night is ordered, he is ordered

the driver's on time. He's taken advice. He keeps his hand
he stays his hand, he can implement...

The boy sleeping under the bridge hears slippers shuffling the bridge
hears a woman's cry. He doesn't move. It could be a ploy.

Procedures. He knows procedures. He knows this track.
He knows the exact, the exact point

to release, to release pressure. The driver's taken advice.
The air is clear. The rails are sharp. He is a man defying the dark.

The man on the bridge hears the train on the track, hears a voice calling,
footsteps dragging. He turns. She is cardigan-ed not white-coated. *Disguised.*

It is February. The air is clear. They are beyond the cemetery.
Beyond fear. The fear on the face of the man in the train of the man in the air.

Incidents in the Travels of an Itinerant Cellist

Fahey believes he is Samson Agonistes
                                        with a cello
that'll rival the horsehead fiddles of Mongolia when he humps it
                                        across the Gobi

giving a nod to Bogdkhan, Tsagaan Nuur and even
        the Darkhad Depression
before its mellow tones bring a smile to Chinngis
                                seated in Sükhbaatar Square.

Fahey knows,
                having consulted the world wide web @ shaggyyak,
                        that courtesy is key
and is prepared to accept the proffered vodka at whatever time,

morning, noon, or,
                but preferably *and*, night, will offer in return
Mal sureg targan tavtai uu?* and a comment on the khavtgai.**

He's a tad uncertain about the consumption
                                of blowtorched marmot
                        knowing the bubonic
is in the handling of their skins especially in August and September.

He'll arrive in July to be on the safe side – being, at the moment,
                                                in transit,
                                                in Belgium.

Next to the Manneken Pis Fahey straddles his cello naked
                                        of thought.
Petite Angelique has passed the hat but tourists are blind
                                to her blandishments,

deaf to the instrument's resonance, attending only to their guide flaunting
                                        his floral umbrella

tied to its purple ribbon, in this labyrinthine city where shades
                                stalk
                        the ornamental
                                in the park
and Hades lies, as Hades must, in the guise of a building
                                        with many stars.

Petite Angelique has led her lover to the Grand' Place.
Beneath her gothic façade she loves to explore the baroque delights
                                        of many layered
                                        petticoats
                                        the pout
                                        of too-pink lips,

the play of light and shade on inner thigh.
In a secret recess she carries Caravaggio.
                        He kisses her behind with every step.
                        Behind her with every step Fahey curses

Purcell,
        his cello,
                Petite Angelique's lover
whose five o'clock stubble sprouts under foundation and powder-pink.

Fahey lusts
            for the chink, ker-chink of coinage. He has travelled so far:
                                                so far
the cents do not amount to a single euro: he dreads a repetition
                                of the Athenian expedition.

At the exact spot
                    that architecte extraordinaire
                Jan von Ruysbroeck landed.
Fahey attempts to transport himself beyond this Place,
                            beyond the eternal quest

for cents and silver, to return to those hallowed days of hangovers
                                    and hymns
                                in the college chapel.

Fahey mourns
                            baguettes and berets,
                            the citizens social charter,
remembers this is Belgium: pigeons and Manneken Pis.
Fahey knows suicide is one option, thrown from the top
                            like Jan von.

A light rain spatters Fahey who wrestles to cover his cello,
                                        resolves to travel
only with a penny whistle if ever he can redeem his reputation.

Dusk. Whispers infiltrate the parc,
            eclipse the earlier call of boys practising moves
showing patience beyond their years as a friend perfects

                    the shoulder roll,
                    the double flick-twist,
                    the double feint
to throw the pursuer, to retain the ball at all costs
                    to pursue a new goal.

Fahey rejects the overtures of M'sieu Lambeaux
                        whose major in Japanese Gothic
allows him to conduct impassioned diatribes on the haut-relief
                                of the Human Passions.

his designs to re-vamp the grand but dusty artefacts
            have been sketched by petite Angelique
whose minor gothic movements Fahey prefers. Fahey knows
                                he and his cello
                                    need
                                    to leave
                                    this city.

* Are your sheep fattening up nicely?
** wild camels.

Passage

We did not know what or who
or why. We only knew.

In that long heat nothing was said
but it hung there

a pinioned crow
for other birds to savage.

Not, as you may suppose
the larger kind but small

sparrows, starlings.
Then there was the thrush.

It's song halted in the pecking.
That remained as unspoken

as where we'd meet each night
once released from our summer jobs

but somehow we'd drift together
first one then another tagging on

aware-unaware
to loaf along the riverbank

where a swan drowned
entangled in a fisherman's cast-offs.

Later, after the last bell-ringer had left
we'd huddle in the churchyard

the night still
still with August heat in the crushed grass

that stained our clothes
or lay with marble cool on our back

where a tee had ridden up.
The marble had its own cold urgency

had names in gold lettering.
We'd trail fingertips

pretend we couldn't see
touch each separate part

trace each curve.
To make letters come alive

the boys said
we need a living model

with a firm stroke, flattering
innocent Eugenie

who wore black
I   ♥   Gravy

emblazoned across her chest.
Eugenie, anxious to please

sang the letters in duet with Rodney.
Was it that night

of that last summer with all those
floating-under-glass feelings

we moved towards reality?
Towards the mute acceptance

in October
of the bursar emptying Eugenie's locker

of the boys, silent and serious
as men now

and Rodney, small and feral
deciding not to be a rock icon

to join Featherstone and Steele
Loss Adjusters.

That summer
the stang of fox was ever-present.

Caravan

Were we other
    we would be a
        single
        straight
        line of camels
        stringing the horizon

      humps bulging or diminished
              depending
in the quest for water
if thirst had been
  slaked.

A serai would be
         appended
yet here
    different appendages apply

    chains
     sunk
into concrete
against inclement weather.

           There is leeway
    but not as saplings
always bending to the wind.

Rocked by the heaviest storm
         still we hold fast
           content now
             not

to drain the day's full measure
            but

to return
to fold into ourselves
to small pleasures
to knowing

that in them
each minute has yielded its own full stretch.

                        Beyond the window
— the cliffs too high to hear the sea —
                                a kayak
the paddle flaying the waves
as if pursued by voices
                by the raconteur of land.
The sea
holds its own consummate might
                                but

with the wash of water
healing salt
    tends
the wound
                    — actual or imagined —

that denies the mind's quiet
                    turning
                        in
on itself.
            Contained.

    We are contained
                        in this caravan
                the pinch and ease of it
compact
in its entirety
all space utilitarian, storage

                        all unwanted matter
                            contained

                as we edge
                awake

a hint of damp ever-present.

Rain thrums the roof
yet the skin will hold fast
no tear, no rent
               despite gulls skid-padding in
               despite their ready-made runway
                    for take-off.

                           We will follow.
                           We will leave
the light blaring our small window
the seethe of rain lifted
                  exposing
                       the shingle spit
                       the rip
alive with seal pup – December born –
                    their small grey faces
                        expectant
                        expectant too

the waves
        furling
      unfurling
the way the surge and ebb of grief
                    engulfs the body

the way it does now
with those seals that are other
                    summer-bearing.

The grunt and wrestle of delivery
precludes males
                bringing with it
the jealous watch/guard of motherhood
                    the fire in the eye

when a camera-click of ferry
                drifts too close.
Aboard
      an old woman gnaws
            the cone's last tapering

                    her tongue seeking sweetness
                    her gums mumbling the ice.
Above
        the sky grey with gulls
                        gull-grey also the sand
                                            shifting
                    the way the old
                                    shift
                                                an easing
of the years' weight
                        the light slant and the eye opaque.

Owen
        fifty years on this coast
        sixty if you count the boy
        unable to handle the river
alone
                        releases his hand on the tiller.
                                        Tomorrow

                        he will take the weight of his father
                                        on his shoulder
the step slow
the ground infirm
from the slur of water.

He will set the coffin
of the oldest river-man
to guide the rudder

                    for a final circle
                    of the seals.

Deference demands the river boat-empty
the quarrel of gulls quietened
the stars exact
                himself uncompassed

yet to learn
        the mastery of tears
                    or how silence floods a crowded room.

                                        Tomorrow
a bell will toll
   binding
the old man
to those who ventured beyond
                        before

their nails rimed with salt
hands slippy with entrails
            with fish, blood fringing the gills
their slither of words
                  sensate.

                  They knew
                  the power and innocence
of steel
the belly slit
the limit of red.

                  In the bones
an ancient knowledge
of quartering
of the stench of flesh

                        fire melting fat
the crowd waiting
while the skin crisps.

      The last gull
            pegs a fish
the lights of the last bus hurry our steps.

Serrated wrack strews the beach
causing us to stumble.
                  You slip
                  your arm into the crook of mine
encompassing the day

                  an unfinished sufficiency.

The Re-Telling

Without light we travelled, bent by snow,
the ice-bite of stars in a flinty sky our typography,
each letter conveying the weight of history:
the genesis of making the unknown, known.

*

Steel-caps know how to make a light history. A shiver
of glass an' mate, the Lecky's *Any person damaging*...
As if we gave a flying fuck. We wanted dark. The alley.
His way home. No way out. He'd pay. He'd know

Don't mess with Joe. Mean. Joe's been with that Mary
a coupla years an' not even dipped his wick. Not bent.
Says in his country a wife comes pure. Virgin. Spotless
Not even thought about it. Thank Christ I live here.

*

We were reluctant to leave. One said the stars were out
of alignment, the second spoke of our other false hopes.
And why leave my new concubine who would weave
intricate patterns on my skin she'd cooled with rose water,
her hennaed fingers, such a pale shade of brown, feeding
me only the finest figs, first drawing that glistening purse
bursting with seed, into her own mouth to moisten before
flicking it on her tongue...Such a tongue. The promise!
The delights to come resonating on its pink tip fluttering
between her lips, those childish lips reddened with passion.

*

Joe's no mincer. Only gotta shake his curls an' the women...
Let's just say they were never girls. Take that first night.
Sight of 'em hunched over his lunch pack. Talk about
share and share alike. None of 'em 've looked back since.

An' the mouths on 'em. They notch up scores in the carsie.
That Mary'll never know. Never see her. Old man keeps her
tighter 'n a duck's arse. 'Cept for Joe. Sundays. Saint's days.
Nutty things like that. He's there. I swear, butter wouldn't melt....

We get a look in then. Not that Joe's lairy with it. No way. Knows.
Show respect or pay. That fairy Gabe'll find out. Don't mess
with a bloke's tart. He shoulda kept to Teresa. Mother Teresa.
She's all heart. Six kids, dozen dads. An' what she does for afters!

*

But this child would be different. The crow's feather laid at each
of our doors, not once but each of three nights, the way the wind
sprang around our palaces yet stilled whenever we ventured out
to consult the stars and the very stars themselves shut their faces,
ceding the desert to the ululations of wolves, whinny of stallions,
their wild manes streaming in terror at the unexpected dark –
yes, we knew. Yet still we refused. Preferred our own pursuits.
But at the failing of all light in the Holy Place and an unknown
peacock, tail ablaze, strutted back and forth before our faces –
we were afraid. To have delayed further would betoken death.
Whose death none could say and none had words as we loaded
camels with oil and grain and gifts. Such gifts. Gifts fit for a King.

*

Mean. Joe's not from round here. Being foreign. Not a turban! Just…
Foreign. But knows to keep stumm when Harold just-call-me-god
comes sniffing 'n' I'm off the job. I've a nice little earner on the side.
Not been rumbled. Though Joe's got a whiff. But no lip, just covers.
And he's a good chippy. So. This little number's a *Thanks, Joe*.

Mel gave me me blade. Nice. Jag-edged. Serrated. Got it in Ibiza.
He'd had a ruck with a coupla local gits. You don't fuck with Mel.
They hopped it faster'n a fart in a colander. Left this. See. It glints.
Gold. Gabe'll appreciate it. Or maybe not. Won't be singing then.
Not if we give him a little cut where he wouldn't show his mother.

Yeah. Little nick there…Be well good. Being what he's done to Joe.
Choir. 'S how Gabe latched onto Mary. So it's only fair we help him
with high notes. Voice like an angel. Posh talk. Posh job. Newsreader.
Trainee. Thatch of blonde hair. Him not her. Got her dad to let him
walk her home nights Joe was …whatever. So reckon we need
to give him something to sing about over the hills and far away.

*

Yes, the journey was hard and often we were quarrelsome,
resenting the loss of our independence in the governance
of our days. We cleansed our selves once, twice, thrice daily
yet still the sand penetrated our robes, hid in the folds of skin
within our innermost parts, our buttocks rubbing sore against
each jolt of camel and the camels themselves, so fractious,
their beautiful eyes plagued by flies, stings suppurating belly,
back, fetlock – it was torture to shackle them during the day
as we slept. Their spit grew venomous. Our words likewise.
Yet we knew each man's wisdom complemented the others'.
We knew also to seek inner solitude in this crowded desert.

*

I've kept well stumm about this little caper. Mel knows. An' Balfy.
His aftershave! Ruddy corpse long dead an' dug up smells sweeter.
Umbelliferous plant, my eye. If his smell gives this rumble away....
Mind. He's an answer for everything. Reckons what I use to calm
me nerves causes me asthma, makes me gasp, so he calls me.
Gasper. He gets sarky, I get narky. But come something like this....
Like brothers. Never mind being mob-handed. Leave that to the rest.
Come the acid test, we're there for each other. We stick like shit.
We all operate our own patch. Our own little kingdom. Our own tarts.
Keep our selves to selves. But when its curtains you call for mates
you can rely on for certain. An' that's Mel. An' me. An' Balfy. Natch.

*

Yet when we were greeted by horseman we drew together as one.
We waited silently. No steel was drawn. We did not possess such.
Our wisdom serves as our weapon. Oh, had we had the wisdom
to refuse the press of these strangers, to choose another direction,
to keep our news close, we would have been spared the ignominy
history has imposed upon us. But I plead, what choice did we have?
Our reputation in the reading of stars had preceded us, the horseman
inviting participation in the delights of the palace were quietly forceful.
After the itch and scratch of desert fleas it seemed sanctuary indeed.
But, in mitigation, know we refused to partake of the king's concubines.

*

Then there's Harold's lot. Does the dirty work for the Eye-ties.
Well geared up. Big knives, small pricks. You keep that stumm!
He'd give me a right bum's rush faster'n you can flick a bogey –
gotta think of me day job. The legit one. I'm no layabout. No way!
Work hard, play hard. Two jobs. And a little night earner with girls.

Till the Eye-ties muscled in. They know how to flank 'emselves
over the manor. Each protecting the other's fanny. Friggin' pain.
They came, fought, set up a chain of command an' moved on.
Harold's their main man here. His business is just a front! Clever!
Ever want to slit your own throat, step out of line. He'll do it for you.
Legit. You'll never work again. He calls the union his army. The git!

*

The star led us to him who would be known King of the Jews.
Others were present. Each paying his dues. The mother shed
the same remote smile on shepherd or goat, camel or king.
Afraid we had been followed we laid our gold, frankincense
and myrrh, made our obeisance and sought another direction
to our land which gave us succour. We will not travel again.

*

Where's that ponce Gabe gone? Bloody choir's well over. He shows
it'll be his ruddy swan song. Reckon he's heard about Joe's bird. Knows
we know who's been walking her home, Sweet talking when she's alone.
The word'll be out on the street we're waitin'. There's no escaping that.
'S a fact of life round here. Eyes out of their backsides some of 'em.
I swear they're aware of every fart or fuck before it's even started.

Too friggin' scared to do anything though. Look at that ruck yesterday.
It was Harold's mob. He heard on the grapevine about some geezer
marking his territory. So he puts out feelers. Comes up with these three
likely lads. They harp on they know what's what. He treats 'em royally.
Booze, birds, blokes, the lot. That was as far as he got. Right prick.
How thick can you be? First chance they scarpered. Left Harold carping.

He's not one to take things lying down. But even for him it was over the top. Once he realised they'd done a runner he had his spies out day an' night, non-stop. Spies know. They wanna live they've gotta come up with the info. Any info. Fast. So they did. Don't rightly know why they chose that actual neighbourhood. Suppose they wanted rid. Harold off their backs. An' he didn't hang around. Swore he'd gun the geezer whoever, wherever he was. But Christ! A child's playground!

from

A Lope of Time

(Shoestring, 2009; reprinted 2011)

Frau Schackenberger's Afternoon

Frau Schackenberger, windows shuttered,
snaps five lever locks top and bottom,
enters the cage that bears her down
and steps into the opera of sirens and horns,
the bird-quick chatter of oriental tourists,
pitter-patter of French, pucker of morphemes,
a whole slop of sounds: the litter of a city
phoenixed from debris. And everywhere the cry,
Bitte, können Sie mir helfen?

But she ignores maps, wordless pointings,
the halt of a language never learnt,
the falsetto request of the burlesque Englishman,
the tug of a child at her close buttoned coat,
moves without care of time or traffic –
For who can curb either one?
Be assured each will take what each will take –
ignores the pedestrian red, the curses, ache of back,
sails across *Bismarckstrasse* to a soprano of brakes.

From this roundabout of roads she turns
into a craze of streets that mourn loss
of discreet hotels where in the small of afternoons
bankers played (but to no profit)
returning empty to wives full of *Kaffee und Kuchen*
(but eaten by the *Kulturforum*) who offer,
from the debris of tissue, boxes and bags,
a litter of tickets to this city's delights,
a smooth back, *Bitte, kannst du mir helfen?*

and the quick click fastens jewels tight:
but who will rise in this new millennium to prise them
from wedding finger, back of tooth, hollow shoe?

Time remembered is time forgotten:
the clutter of carts on crowded roads,
neighbours, strangers, leaving cities,
a steady rhythm of border-bound trains,
whispers of smoke from brick-built chimneys,

chimneys such as a craftsman would make
and he might live in your town or village,
next door's son or cousin's nephew,
never your own, Yahweh, never your own!

But neighbour Frieda has bread. Bread, brown not grey
and what is seeping in the napkin? Meat, maybe?
And where is her Jakob? He who could build walls
higher than trees, for whom is he working?
And why would she rather spend Sabbath alone?
Father, a gentle man of slow courtesies, refused her wine,
swung his youngest shoulder high and with shaven head,
hair bleach and humour entered this city littered with rumours,
to watch high kicking men in a time of recession
crave of the saviour – *Können Sie uns helfen?*

Frau Schackenberger shakes her head in disbelief
at the puny saplings that clutter this street, longs for the limes
on *Unter den Linden* when flags and singing promised tomorrow
to father and child. They'd cheered, waved Liesl, a doll with real hair,
– whose hair she didn't know – but knows now
there are no maps to memory: the lamp that spills its light
on familiar joys attaches unsuspected spurs of sorrow:
they'd called on Christ, an unknown god not the god of the Torah,
the god of Chanukah whose candles she'd counted,

who'd blessed the table before father's audacity
in coming to this city without letters or luggage
where now she wanders doubly dispossessed:

a convert, lapsed, cannot reclaim her abandoned history
borne in bones, such bones as bore yellow stars
that littered the camps: beyond belief, beyond *Bitte, helf mir.*

A stealth of snow touches her face – the face of a woman
who has never traced the silky-clean cheek of her child.
She steps into cafe-dark as Otto, outflanked by Helmut's pipe
and a phalanx of salt cellars, counter-attacks with pepper pots,
yanks a check-cloth-Alps in a war, lost but never admitted

— look at this city phoenixed from debris — while from the litter
of napkins and knives, Heinrich's soft, *Kann ich Ihnen helfen?*
He seats her at a table for one, adjusts his gold-wired glasses
to loss and custom, cuddles the three-legged cat for comfort.

Frau Schackenberger muses on the menu, chooses
what she will not order though a tip's in her purse,
for services and salutations exact compensation, always
a price to pay in this city where the Wall has fallen
and unlicensed taxis like taxes, multiply. *Unification is fine*
as a fishbone in the throat. Street-smart graffiti litters this city.
Gone the accordion player who sweated over buttons and bellows
while a nation, joyous in beer gardens, claimed their destiny
in a fire that's faded to the heat of Helmut and Otto's murmurs.

Frau Schackenberger shakes free of memory, places one old *Pfennig*
beneath the cloth, levers herself from table to table, routs Otto's Alps,
grates open the door and eases out into a sift of snow.
She will return to that part of the city where women in black
talk endlessly of Krakow under drifts of trees on this *Platz* or that.
She scatters coins into a disused doorway, misused by drunks or whores,
but the hunched form does not stir, sleeps on in a stench not his own.
The ache in her back joins the pain in her heart but she ignores
the gape of U-bahn, seeks safety on a bench to gather her strength.

Such accidents of time or place in unremembered times,
a tangle of names that had to be changed, a word drumming
in her blood, a word reviled, relived in rehearsed memories...

Frau Schackenberger sits on in an alteration of light.
undisturbed by tourists who travel from Tiergarten
to Charlottenburg in a landscape of sounds, of words unknown.

Frost-filaments glee her hair. In the still of this long dark
footsteps fade: a dog raises his leg by hers. She hums,
Under the Judas Tree but no sound comes not even *Hilf.*

While Waiting For Bad News

April is the cruellest month...

T.S.ELIOT

1

How can one letter weighing only a few grams
hold so much time suspended?

What have they not told you?
What have I not?

* * *

You are my *Seven Sisters*
walked in snow and rain,
my winter sun hanging low
in a ragged sky.

Sweeter than the apple in the attic
stored till winter's end you are
the pasture where lions and lambs lie
the garden in which the wren rests.

Where will I run to, where hide
when winds rip trees from roots,
boats from moorings? Why, to you,
my anchor, my anchor.

2

Yet how did we start?
How could I have known love?

I had only the word for it
and tears did not come easily.

> I was the poppy blazing red
> your blaze of red, your stain
> > your runnel of blood

> you were the pull of the moon
> the shadow in the night
> my darkness and my light

> I was the day to your moon
> the sun to your night
> the burn of your day.

Yet water on stone
was not slower in its siege
than your constancy.

3

What eclipse let love steal across my sky?
      I did not see it.

What word was brushed from your lips to mine?
      I did not feel it.

What prayer was whispered in cathedral dark?
      I did not hear it.

But the smell of salt whipped on wind that tears
      your hair, your skin and the taste....
            God, the taste of you!

4

Were you a bird I'd eat the skin, bone, feathers of you.

Though I would save one bone, one feather,
not as a keepsake for that would be within me,
– having gorged your strength, your gentleness –
but to make a mark on clay or cuneiform, papyrus
or paper, use your bone to press keys, your iridescent
feather for a quill to form letters in the old way.

The alphabet of days is lodged in you
without you there is no holy Sunday
only Wednesday's child, full of woe.

Where will I take my sorrow?
The house cannot hold it
and the garden has its own rue.

5

Is there no prayer, no novena
to chant at Lourdes or Fatima,
no cockleshell in hat at Compostela?

If Easter comes early will Taxco
be empty, Seville's mountains
not thrum to resurrection drums?

What will I do now for my fool in April?
Why will you leave your fool in April?

When the children chant
Spring forward, Fall back
What am I to do?

Notes on a Journey

The Friends' Café closes shortly.
Later:

The vending machine needs 50p's.
Its cups need care, they disintegrate at touch.

But what is whole?
The crisp-clean touch and turn
of medics
inserting a catheter –   an addition
to your molecular composition?

Half a mile of corridor
from here

a man
slides
a body

carefully
onto
the slab

another – green capped, scrubbed –
takes a knife
to discover what lies behind death.

He will be particular
in this   particular death
distinct
from any other
– o, the wound may be the same
but was, is, the journey?

The chocolate's synthetic and the cold cans, aren't.

But there is chill enough
in this precision of language
which holds
no fear
that a slipped scalpel may   pierce the soul.
Or has that left with death?

If so are you still whole
though there's barely a poh-poh
or pulse-beat under your sheet?

                                    I cannot find you!

Where is my guardian, my angel of light?
Where is the reassuring hand
                         the dispeller of night's mares
                         the fingers that held tight
the spatula
levelling my tongue that I may breathe?

I will breathe with you, for you.
In   out   in
                      my hand
your dry bones.

A flake of skin clings to my fingers.

                    Time is no longer measured
in past or present
only in the dimming of lights
                  after
the night trolley
            has passed us by –

                  after
the old woman has climbed
               three times
                            out

the other side
        of the bed
where the nurse has – three times –
           placed her
           and the old man
gropes – again – for the bottle
           between his legs.

Is this all that is left of the incessant chase?
Youth wanting age firmly in place
                           age wanting escape?
Bottles at the beginning, middle, end of life?

    Imprisoned
                                 in glass
a silhouette dangles
                  a stethoscope   mouthing   at me
jerking a stubbled chin   towards a side room   where I
                                                         will not follow
                                                         will not discuss death.

Your guiding hand covered
              my child-hand
and now mine holds yours.
              If I let go you may
                           let go.

Beyond the glass
              a penthouse. Its height
lending uncurtained windows
              a privacy
not known here
where cubicle curtains
                   never   quite   close.

Formed crab-wise to you I feel
                           proprietary
hands trying to ease
              us   apart.
                           I'm ordering you
a cab. You'll feel better for a proper sleep.

Her bottom clenches in retreat.
                           Too tired
to argue, she wants a comforting bath,
                           strong G&T.

And me.
        What do I want?
        For you to return?
        For you to be.....

not this body

          alcohol-rubbed
          skin tissue-d
          thinned by years

not this body

            whose weight a nurse eases
                single-handedly.

                      She leaves
mouth swabs by the sputum pot
                no
brass bowl to offer food to gods
                   disinfectant
                   not incense
will communicate with the after life.

            Changing shift
nurses exchange concerns
re-visit the admission form
     note
alone in house with patient

                   note
*?NAI**

                   note
Why the constant vigil?

         Their faces blear
towards our bed
(the one nearest the door)

                   note
the body must go straight to....

half a mile of corridor

from here
                   where a man
                        – green capped, scrubbed –

will be particular
in this particular death
                                 distinct

from any other.

* Non-accidental injury

from

Where Acid has Etched

(bluechrome, 2007)

East coast looking eastward

If I draw a line from here to your shore,
then take the tram …

You remember the tram?
The station? Where the woman paced,
her pram empty
and each face discarded,

where the light hung
sulphur yellow and the phlegm
of the seaman
split the air between us
and with the parting, the departing:

where rain-stricken streets
guttered the blood and the shaft
of the knife
licked clean, gleamed

into the candle-dark
basement as coffee, slopped
in thick bowls,
bittered the tongue
hastening the parting, the departing:

where urgent cries
in endless alleys ceased
as a clatter of coins
scattered the rats
parting and passing, never departing.

* * * * *

Parting and passing, never departing
the women sashay, lounge to kitchen,
kitchen to stair and from there….
But Rena's watching. Watching

arrival kisses exchanged with care
(the air has never been pouted so much)
exquisite cheeks laid side by side:
only for the intimate a butterfly touch

and not for Little Eva
who carries their coats, places,
replaces plates of foie gras.
Her child-hands pour wine

that clings to thin glass rims
raised in expectations,
unspoken, understood but easily denied
for they've never been spoken.

Over the music words rise and fall.
Under the guise of a slow hiss
of smoke, a kiss is puckered
across the table, is caught in the droop

of an eye. There's nothing to disturb
this room of trivial talk:
if silence disturbs, it's curbed
in the swish of satin on silk. And still

Little Eva flits with roulades of sushi,
blinis and brie, enough to hush the harshest
laugh as her hump back shrinks back
the women who wait, gorge, watch

Rena watching. Who will be first
to pass beyond kitchen to stair
and dare to mount? To delight
into the stranger's ear a snare

of promises, already forgotten
in the long rip of zip down silk,
a tease of fingers and soft cries
denoting the parting, not departing.

* * * * *

In the dark trams depart,
slipping over rails sleek as leaves
steeped with rain,
past alleys obliquely set,

past small hotels
where wires uncoil from sockets
in wardrobeless rooms.
Here the taliped seaman mocks

the memory of a mother
never known but paid in every dock.
This time she doesn't move.
The stain on the counterpane

is already drying as he takes
his pain beyond lighted windows
where a hunchback slips swift as a knife
and a woman watches.

* * * * *

A line of light drops
down the hill, steel tears steel
as it stops, shudders, begins again
towards that same station

in an endless ring of rail
that we also rode.

When you say... *Dance?* you should know.......

Last light. The shadow falls across the wall
where sunlight flickers its own graffiti
over graffiti's air-brushed promise
Gary wil allways lov Denise xx.
Stone kisses caress but the flinty kiss
of a sated lover transported me and nothing
remained but to move on to some other dance.

Empty coal trains clattered the night.
Snow clouds hung yellow over a river
leaked with light: passing barges discharged oil
that streaked her blonde hair, glossed lips,
swollen but not from kisses, and rimmed nails
that crazed a bare back all New Years day when we
remained to move to some other dance.

That summer rain slashed tenements of gulls
that wreathed every pitch and pot of houses
without guests. Pensioners slacked by a dun sea
under an ugly sky. Each clump of rocks the hunch
of her back as I crabbed sand between bare toes,
drew guilt close as a caul around what sadness
remained before moving onto some other dance.

Europe misted memory. A thumb primed at 90 degrees
made lorries shudder dust on mountain roads
where old currency — breasts half tamed in a halter top,
his seed, prolific as pomegranates' —
bartered in the humming dawn and words —
whose words? in which language? — told that despair
remained: had moved into some other dance

But some languages are not for sharing
so we skimmed countries silently, pointed
out stone and rocky places, avoided.
burst tyres, shattered headlights. Visa-less,
India stayed unvisited — but what visa grants
safe passage from memory? — Albania, closed,
remained so as we moved from each other's dance.

Alone, all roads became cross-roads. Each road
a country: each country merely a road.
Yet still the body moved till gradually
Greece beckoned, offered sheep's eyes and Matala stew —
wild onions, grasses, herbs strewn amongst bones
left by lepers before travellers came,
remained, then moved on to some other dance.

If history lies in ancient remains
what history remains in ancient lies?
Leave historians to screen, carbon date,
determine what is to be determined,
a scream, unseen, unheard, terminates
more than one life: this you should know before
you air-brush our graffiti, take my hand
and move these remains in some other dance.

Helen

i.m.

We had pipes not drums, four dykes to carry the coffin
and a woman vicar who couldn't pronounce Fuengirole,
where you had your bar bought and sold before the Costa
became packaged and you came home to where mannikins
mixed with mannequins and a sequin was for sewing not singing.*

Dykes in those days were deemed bargain basement.
Wooden stairs precipitated down to Dodge
who took our money and not offence, and to Deena,
who, with foot long holder and cards neatly splayed,
re-captured wages from barstaff foolished into five card stud.
Driving home, first gear, two wheels on the pavement
We're driving at a pedestrian pace, officer
and up 3 a.m. uncarpeted stairs, smoothing rizlas,
Dylan and Donne until dawn – and you out to drive the 27
and me in the Robin Reliant bunny hopping the road –
Jesus, Helen, God must've wanted us living
No, hen, He was too bloody scared to invite us up there.

We'd cake walk the King's Road sunshined before us,
crossing to kiss Zelda who trod the tightrope in spangled jumpsuit
and died in the dust of some Afghan plain:
over again to sashay past Picasso's, desperate for Tanya or Scarlett
to admire your Beetle jacket, a decade out of date
but worn with pride by you, fresh from the Costa via
the WRAF escape route from a Scottish village
to lipstick lesbians, deconstructionism and the Kitchen
where one sauce served all dishes but with a litre of wine
there'd be change from a fiver and we'd be pigeon-toeing
centre road to press Polish Helen's hand as she gazed at the bars
of the barracks for a glimpse of that father whom she'd never recognise,
who'd shed other things along with his shiny demob suit –
no words to compensate for her childhood camps,
her mother in their one basement room rocking; rocking ...

By the time Sisters were doing it for themselves, we'd done it
and for us it was always *Mama* who had the brand new bag
so when did you sell out for proper jobs and pension rights?
Trade greeting cards not kisses? Settle for slippers not slappers?
Whatever. This is for you, Helen, and that other Helen
who, New Year's Eve, threw herself from Battersea Bridge
to be dragged four month river swollen
back to where we all, alone, walked our own walk.

* *Sew on a Sequin* by Fascinating Aida

47

Generations

Three times today the snow has fallen.
Now, the windows shuttered, the house blind,
all is silent except for the wind
that haunts the chimney, sifts ash that patterns
careless scrolls on a carpet where the child
pauses in play, cuffs a sudden tear,

hides it from eyes that also know tears.
Three times today the snow has fallen
and each time a mother has watched her child
raise his face to catch the soft damp, raise blind
eyes as snow light frets bare branches, patterns
them on yellowed skin, once roughened by wind

scouring childhood hills far from fields where wind
brought fear. There, shrapnel savaged men tear
gas had blinded. There, you could trace patterns
of rats' feet on bodies glazed by fallen
snow. Men hung on wire while bullets, blind
to prejudice, sniped flesh as the child

will snip a head or foot from his child's-
story book or throw play punches that wind
his father – an unerring fit for blind
man's buff. In his part-face, two holes. No tears
can fall. He has no word for the fallen
snow. No words on which to thread the pattern

of his day as on his raised face, patterns
of flakes melt. A mother watches her child.
A child watches his father, wipes fallen
snow lodged in empty sockets, pretend wind
tunnels. The child blows. The snow melts, forms tears.
The child smiles. His grandmother knows he's blind

with grief but refusing to cry. The blind
man cannot feel his mother's rage that patterns
all her days. She smiles, takes the child's hand. Tears
are for private times. She protects the child
who protects her. They listen to the wind.
The child draws stick men belly-up, fallen

on snow. The blind man dribbles. The child
bayonets patterns in stick men, blames wind
for tears. Three times today snow has fallen.

from

The Silence Unheard

(Shoestring, 2013)

Witness

We had heard the dove's three notes and seen
the curve of light against a naive sky, smelt

unguent from crushed palms beneath our feet
and were caught between hosanna and crucifixion.

Knowing what was written we were afraid
of what might be demanded, wary of that we might discover

beyond birth. So, yes, we did travel slowly, each decision
an indecision, each suggestion once, twice, questioned

but at the first snow-melt we began our journey,
followed rivers in full flood from the abundance that ice

had borne through winter's keep, had, at the hint
of a reluctant spring, chosen, if choice were possible,

release. Of course, dying framed the silence.
There was the call of one reaching out for the comforting

cry of another, the hand held, a touch,
though all were beyond the reach of language, beyond

those small hypocrisies of death. The first true birth.
The knot cut close.

For what is the past but the scar of other centuries, a spike
of time to beat against locked doors? And who will dare

to open to the stranger whose words are differently chosen,
whose promise is exemption? Yet, unhope,

framing the silence, clings tight as a caul and krumholz*
smothers abandoned gardens

where those who have sown thought falter. Perhaps,
only the blind man, he who rocks at the edge of the known,

his world a long cane's length, may pierce those dark tangles,
may witness what is written.

But who would believe in the word of the unseeing?
Or know in the unseen is the silence unheard?

Though when the bleed of shadow behind the sun
darkened the sky

we held fast to the charred end of that day,
knew the cry was the pith reluctant to release the flesh.

And still we failed, unprepared
for linen unwound, the re-composition, sheltered by stone.

* krumholz – dark tangles of dwarf hemlock

On Being Presented With A Painting
Of Buffaloes In The Snow

Snow did not stop us nor the long trek,
the mountain's ridge constant at our backs.

Oh, we were not skilled, had not studied maps,
contours, but we knew the way of men, of stars,

though we remained wary. One of us remembered
the lash of a bullwhip on a back already red,

the ropes chafing raw places as log after log
added to the load. Another spoke of our virility, our horn,

being wrested from a brother only half dead, his bellow
choked in the dust as they stood on his matted head —

yes, we knew the ways of men, knew the potions
they contrived in the name of love. So when we heard

the stars had said a man would carry logs equal
to our own, we blared with laughter. Yet disbelief

is not our nature. Each contemplated the matter,
our thoughts slowing our steps in the rough of harness,

drawing down such savagery as even we had not known.
That decided us. Conference was brief — men are afraid

of our restlessness, our talk, and we have experience
of what that means. So we finished the season, dragging

timber behind us until the snows came when men cringed
in their byres but left us to roam, to fend for ourselves.

We waited until the river almost froze yet was fluid enough
for us to cross, our coats glittered, sharp with night-ice.

Come morning, all would be ice yet the river's thin crust
would not bear the weight of man, would close over his head.

And so we remain resolute. We are not reluctant journeymen.
We will seek the one who is born to haul crossed logs.

If true, he will make history and he could be one of us.
Indeed, we have heard that he too needs shelter.

Why leave it to lambs, an odd donkey or two, our half-brethren
the cows and bulls — our breath is as warm as theirs.

Notes While Waiting

The day barely breathing
along the long sigh of corridors
with closed doors.

Defaced by creases and crayons
the spotted laminate of Patient-Partnership
slips to the floor.

Unaware, in-coming patients peel away
to an appropriate department whose signs
are infallible

oncology, radiology, surgery

leaving coffee half drunk in Styrofoam cups
leaving debris the porter will later remove.

* * * * *

The consultant refuses to be drawn –
persistence elicits
he is not a prophet

But John too cried in the wilderness
I am not the one ye seek

He scrawls a note, each word incisive
caps his fountain pen, bows, opens door
and there is the corridor.

This lift for medical personnel only
And the doors glide shut.
Patients shuffle to the next where men

caged in metal, whistle, remove
the blanking plate
search, discard, insert, screw back the cover

and leave, laughing, nudging one another
at the nurse's bum
as she sashays along the corridor

to enter the door
– her thoughts not strictly medical –
of Mr. Jordan, surgeon, who is buffing his nails.

Thereupon Jerusalem and all Judea
went to see him, to confess their sins
and he

accepts the sheaf of notes
politely professional to his fingertips
but examines that same part of her anatomy

as the engineers and sighs, opens the door
onto the long corridor
onto the inward eyes of the sick

and when he saw these, he asked
Who was it that taught you, brood of vipers,
to flee from the vengeance that draws near?

Hospital No: 030445AKA – the patient –
slides his eyes from his boots
still fertile with soil from the site

upon which he and Mr. Wimpey will build
the New Jerusalem –
sidles across parquet flooring and whispers

shut the door
dividing sanctum from corridor
diagnosis from prognosis.

Already the axe has been put to the root of the tree

Now Mr. Jordan bathes him in the light
of his computer, indicates the negative
showing positive. Hospital No: 030445AKA

has no need to undress any more
simply to listen while unfamiliar words
wash over him. Practised in the art

of denying the D…. word, Mr Jordan
ushers him smoothly through the door
his over-sized boots stumbling the corridor

one will come after me who is mightier than I,
so that I am not worthy
even to carry his shoes

to the pub, to his mates, who determine
from his glazed state that he's already had enough.
Which he has.

Later, the porter, having removed the debris
will prop that same bar in that same spot
but will not know who or what has gone before.

It's not his grind. The union'd be on his back
if he did more than separate domestic
from clinical. One he chutes

but the chaff he will consume with fire
between hands of stud in the basement
while he waits for the final call from above.

The chaplain waits by Recovery
for one long-known
yet long since lost. Along the back corridor

the rattle of empty metal, thrusts through the door
— rubber, for ease of access.
The exit will be silent, the long box weighted now

as the porter hums his way
on this last journey of his day. He winks at a nurse
bids goodnight to Mr. Jordan who nods and smiles

as he strides toward the room
of his consultant colleague, ready for a snifter
whilst discussing the latest case. Liver.

The consultant demurs. He has a new wife.
He pulls in his stomach
recalls the new Director's post, acquiesces

and draws his garment of camel's hair
and a leather girdle about his loins.

       * * * *

In the grounds
a leaf–skeleton is tossed
by an adventitious wind

that carries
the *chek-chek* of a squirrel
seeking a mate.

Smoke rises from the grey building
on the left – the re-cycled packed in ice
has already left. On the right

an organ releases compressed air.
The chapel's dampness
clings to the chaplain's robes.

Audit

In this small garden, held ransom by a wren,
the red of azaleas deepens, handsome
camellias proffer porcelain blossoms
while a far-off, scratchy, *Je ne regrette rien*
tussles with the noise of starlings repeated
cries in the graveyard beyond our wall.
Such imagery may be the sirens' call
to darker thoughts but perhaps a discreet
silence should still prevail – let us prevent
disruption of the years' collusion: sense
withheld in the face of all evidence.
Oh, yes, we were, are, our own testament
to what we sought, however big, however small:
did we seek only what pleases, ignore what appals?

Did we seek only what pleases, ignore what appals?
Such traits prove fertile ground, inciting deaths –
Arabs, Jews, blacks or Kurds, the dispossessed –
anyone whether persuaded, enthralled,
enticed (intimidation is simply
the first resort.) *Not me! Not in my name!*
No? How does it differ when you felt shame
at a lover's faux pas and turned primly
to cross the room? Easy to disengage
when the wind is in the wrong direction.
Is love merely the flotsam and jetsam
encountered in a day's trawl to assuage
fear of endless afternoons? The lover
turning his velvet cheek to your iron glove?

Turn the velvet cheek to the iron glove?
Our history proves a salutary
lesson. War or love, celebratory
blessings soon give way to the push and shove,
the manipulation of that abstract
– Truth. Whether one's name is Kelly or Christ
there's a B. Liar spouting imprecise
information – but don't over re-act!
It's all there. Documented by his friend –
Oh, for a burning Bush in the desert!

Useless for millions to march to subvert
such political intent. Condemn
us if you will but remember the damned:
Mai Lai. Sarajevo. Dafur. Basra. Vietnam.

Mai Lai, Sarajevo, Dafur, Basra, Vietnam
curl them on your tongue as salacious age
deserts Old Compton Street in days when Aids
is an unfortunate fashion and dam-
nation is delivered with the news. Truth
or lies? Will those who lie with truth heal scars,
beat breasts: *mea culpa, mea culpa?*
No – but add maxima to the name *Ruth.*
How many chance fires, stoked, were left to smoulder?
Dressed in summer's night rain, curtained windows
remained closed against the day's gaudy show.
Now the sun no longer leans on my shoulder,
restless spring shrivels into autumn's husk,
winter comes: park gates close against the dusk.

Winter comes, park gates close against the dusk,
a moon's steely light silvers distant trees
whose branches scrawl their own calligraphy.
Solitary footsteps crush snow but musk
from a mistress lingers, discreet, in suburbs
where marriages, trimmed to perfect politeness,
prepare for night. Duvet-ed Carmelites toss;
disciplined Benedictus burns, curbs
desire for *millefeuille* served by *Mam'selle*
Angelique in the small shop where roads cross.
Direction determined by a coin's toss
creates strange alliances, forms cartels;
pockets chink-chink with promise, cents, artful,
oil grief – undermines the woman in Kabul.

Grief undermines the woman in Kabul,
burkha-clad, whose husband drools in shadow
from his part-face to a fine concerto
of Kalashnikovs; let's grant criminal
compliance in our silence. While she claws

close a plastic bag – her son's flesh – we seek
sanctuary in whatever keeps bleak
reality at bay. Let us ignore
her despair, feed our desire – the antidote
that muffles the lone beat of the nearing drum.
To those for whom death is the only plum,
give; to deaden guilt we slip a large note
into the thin Christian Aid envelope.
Strange how your world and mine has telescoped.

Strange how your world and mine has telescoped.
Omniscient with youth we staged lock-outs/
sit-ins, dodged water cannon, the draft. Doubts
denied, we flew our ragged flag of hope.
Now we wait for a sullen sun to touch
limbs that once quivered at thought. How we long
for the sharp bark of fox – his evensong
spurred our lust – yet even as we watch
for a new moon, the light wanes and unnamed
parts yearn only the cool of cotton sheets.
In night's heat we rake embers of past, fleet
affairs – friends, lovers – declare, unashamed,
fidelity, take our ease at last when
in this small garden, held ransom by a wren.

WRINGING BLOOD

Antecedent

Those kisses you placed upon my cheek
first left then, adroitly, right, were formal
as an English handshake upon greeting
upon leaving behind.

                And you, uncertain
loath to go, unable to say what lies between
swoop, catch the corner of my mouth, naked
                               eyes open.

                Behind lies
the late night ferry pulsing in safe harbour
Barreiro's distant lights waiting to welcome.
I wanted wilder waters and you.

In Absentia

Vital this opening. You mail from Lisbon and my silver
Apple conveys the news. Outside, the pointed cypress
pierces a skin of sky, of cloud while, waiting, mist falls
the way the unexpected contracts all to the immediate.

Distance deters contact. Stricken, I know we cannot be
fellow travellers but knowledge is never acquiescence.
In that dark place silence ruled: we never owned a song
that may chance from some balcony, the woman unseen

behind blue bougainvillea. We had only currency spent
in days, months, years apart – a part is less than whole
so I will gather you to me, give you the narrative I travel.
We will elude all others. In our winter, this is our spring.

2.

Here it is spring. We live in different seasons. Indifferent
seasons have passed but now your mail is a promised
slice of light read beneath this close-closed cypress.
We too will be close but not closed nor sway, as it does

in the slightest wind. Ineluctable, we will refuse confined
spaces. Our time has passed: we have only the remnant.
Let there be no regret but let us not be makers of myths
lest we become victims, once again, to old proscriptions

barred, this time, by our own creation. Unplanned talk
unmasks. We will deny all casuistry with uncorseted
words until we both quiver — taut as bow-touched strings
my tongue plucking each place where you rush for refuge.

3.

Your mail was such an emissary invading familiar
places with tangles from a distant time. Unravelled
memory colludes with imagination, freed of edicts

others dictated. Now *we* will be collaborators, familiar
to each other as a folded map in green waxed jacket:
I claim the navigator role!
                              This is our time to seize all.

Unbound by time or place, we will dismantle parameters
patient as the gardener who waits out winter's long dark
for one shoot to disclose signs of a coming spring.

My mind takes hold as shoulder to shoulder we cross
continents, traverse mountains not yet discovered, range
across roads that may lead to unknown destinations

pursue paths that peter out, delight in gardens, cupolas
cathedrals, the fifteen towers of San Gimignano, drink
wine in Montepulciano, climb in hill towns until we fall

asleep under some Madonna's watchful eye, touching
sole to sole.
              Forgive the weak pun but laughter binds
as surely as your religion though you will insist we visit

Duomo del Santa Maria Assunta, Santa Maria della Scala,
trip into Piccolomini Biblioteca, Porta del Cielo, Poggibonsi
and I choose Margate.
                      Margate? Did I not mention laughter?

4.

There is no toast in Siena like the rubber and butter
beloved of Margate landladies. You've been denied
their coarse cries riding *Dreamland*'s scenic railway
never witnessed the theme park's gradual decline
only to be rescued — *did I mention I married?* —
renamed and become the White Knuckle
(surely all pleasure should be unalloyed)
— *she has given me much joy* — but I
have carried you with me, shared
our love, my sorrow. You buried
memory, I lived it, mixed divinity
in the ordinary, piety's profanity
with coarser cries than those
heard from that same roller
coaster that now exists
re-generated in
Re-imagined
Dreamland.
Toast?

5.

Without, burnt earth reflects brown-bright
as the evening's dusk lends its last light
to shimmer unripe olives in this Tuscan air quick

with birds. Our bus rolls through the cleavage
of hills, not Housman's blue remembered ones
(such blue remembered hills!) but lightened by

a flick of hares kick-boxing in mad-March spring.
Headlights shine into our darkness. We are coming
soon to riverless Siena where the water is constant.

In another place the cracked earth yields its roots.
In another place, taller, erect, you stood over me
your shadow falling exactly on mine, travelling beyond.

6.

How soon you have become a citizen of Siena
striding through tourists and traffic as if born
within this walled city where ancient conflicts

unfurl many banners of few colours: uneasy
alliances sought in Piazza del Campo's heat
assure *Palio* victory. Only *Lupa* walks alone.

Lupa is our *contrada* – I refuse to walk alone.
I have carried you with me, hidden in decades'
confusion: the last glass of wine never enough.

7.

I say

Such cheek to refer to poets
only by name of their *porta*

Smiling, you ask why I smile.
Unwilling to say I, smiling, lie
back against warm walls,   lie
in the surety that you will not
smile if you knew how inapt
would be my name, *'Ovila'* .

                    She-wolves
guard 'the sober man'. 'Ovila'
translates into 'the sober man'
translates into this city's gate,
our gate, through which you/I
may escape the walls of old
confined as we are to a past
whose nascent betrayal lies
not in that confessed freely
but that repressed – smiling.

8.

You tell me how the bees your father kept, swarm
form a new colony when unable to sustain desire

for a sovereign remote since winter's huddle: the hive
unable to sustain the warm spring increase, conceive

a new queen leaving the old to seek, with loyal subjects
a different residence without dwelling on her past.

I tell you how my Grandmother died playing football,
not premier league, you understand, but from her chair,

never failing to retrieve, return. She lacked any desire
to die as other old declare they're ready, so we struggled

to keep the balloon floating between us: light as our words
relating insignificant incidents within these Sienese walls.

And then we talk of love, the impermanence of desire:
ignore our accidental rub of shoulder against shoulder.

9.

Shoulder to shoulder they stood: a funnel for prayer
refusing to be routed despite the shattered glass
that once stained avid faces raised in petition.

A fireman, his mouth tight, miserly with secrets,
carried out a marble pieta, the gentle hand cupping
Christ's head the way a midwife fondles the fontanelle.

* * * * *

Shoulder to shoulder we stood: cowled Dominicans' undiluted
black absorbed light: at each discovery prayers circled: each
shift uncovered more bodies under the Basilica's rubble.

The video screen rained snow, signalling the end.
We murmured commiserations for their loss, noted blank faces
noted how their crosses knifed into palms: fingers wringing blood.

10.

The blackest of black is blue, you said. Penance is given
in suffering. I knew only that to imbue rough cloth,

– for it was the Dominicans' darkness you denied –
with exalted attributes, fused the spiritual with material –

fused this second weak pun with understanding the shadow
behind the shadow
                    where crabbed past is a reliquary

sheltering present perceptions.
                    Your thoughts are polished as are
gravestones but you fear the scratch that another may place

upon the coffin in which dispatched emotion festers. Recognition
is not a sin: recall of a temporal time leads to you being blue

the blackest of black. I will wear white, reflect sunlight not swelter
under this Tuscan sun that burns my skin to ebony.
                        If I am ebony
you are stone, both durable yet even granite is porous to a degree.

11.

Have I been harsh? I said there would be no refuge
no respite from reality. We are hostage to our knowledge.

Even the sun adopts the warder's stance, secures us
to shade, our shadows no longer visible. Yet we are craven

willing to cross and re-cross the baked paving to admire
a Fra Angelico, Michelangelo in some small chapel yet refrain

from contemplating living pictures vivid behind eyelids
thinned by sun, by age. We are no longer young. We cannot be

touched by the dead. Let us sew them a new shroud to bury
old suspicions: their mouths' incontinence dribbling lies: for closure.

They cannot hold you, hold us, in thrall if you believe words
staked to this page bear true witness. Do not ask me to draw with water

that no mark of love will be left. We have paid our dues.
We are shriven. I will take the tire from your eyes, give you laughter.

12.

Tumbling from the bus we whoop Poggibonsi! Poggibonsi?
Cheek-trickles of laughter bounce off guarded shops.
Sleeping pigeons shift in the church tower as we swoop
over the campanile, leap over coping separating secular
from sacred ground. Halted by a clock's midnight tolling
through the town, we watch the disappearing tail lights
of our last chance to reach Siena.

You, who have never
ventured beyond the dark of the day except to perform
pre-dawn Lauds, settle down by a flank of wall, balance
our day, already yesterday, against having only moon light
to cover us covering these stones: we lie listening, waiting
for a first twitter of birds – for sounds we cannot yet name.

13.

I gave you a book of birds but they were from a different continent.
I gave you a blue jumper too heavy for summer and not winter wool.
I gave you a curved boning knife, keenly honed. It sliced your hand.
I gave you a disc, Amália, *fadista, Rainho do Fado*, you had no player.
I gave you a flower found in a field of corn, you looked away.
You gave me a map where truth lay lying:
                        I send my poem to where truth lies dying.

14.

Rooted in life we never spoke of death
harnessed each day to the task in hand
marked our narrow life with simple words
selected from a mandatory tract: to elude
authority we transformed their meaning
into cryptic messages.
                                 There was nothing
cryptic, nothing erotic, sent to my silver *Apple*
just plain fact to be read, re-read, re-read....

I printed it, twisted the paper to dislodge
words not wanted. No desire left, I slept
gripping it the way a child falls asleep
holding an empty glove which love
once filled, knowing absent fingers
                                 are his fault.

15.

That night the dark fell heavily as an old curtain
loosed from its rail. Laden from years of neglect
dust choked — a cry rising but caught in the throat:
the throat closing the way a great beast seizes
savages insensate, denying even the last rasp.

16.

Unmoored, I resort to distant days when distraught cries
blocked our path. A fledgling, beak wide open reveals bare
yellow of throat — knowing despair yet too naive to know
endgames come in unexpected places — its *dweep dweep*
on my urban ear strapped my feet securely as a lion's roar.

Country born, you simply said, *Poison pellets* and I, appalled,
sought a solution finding none in your retreating back: heard
Kindness would be to kill. No inflection. Acceptance essential.

The rock, exact in my palm, freed the bird.
                                        There was absence:
the blood and the water not apparent: only the complexity
of silence.
                Without turning, your hand, fine-veined, gripped mine.

17.

Night's stain invades the light, windows deflect the dark
the way widows deflect grief until finally absence breaks.

Absence hollows my mind. Boned of speech, I wait out
a monochrome of days, a waste of days distinguished only

by the clack of tongues tourists spit. Saturdays it's Japanese,
rummaging amongst racks of Armani, Prada, Versace, D&G.

Monday/Tuesday older Italians arrive to jostle with Chinese
leaving mid-week for British who refuse all guidance, spend

unknown afternoons stricken with heat, wanting small
currencies of purchase, bargains to brag back home

with tales of drains, the sloe-eyed waiter. Interlopers,
they gather into bars, onto terraces, sip spritzers, grimace

over rough chianti as shadows lock the Piazza del Campo:
the year is too early for the *Palio*, too early for death.

18.

You are enclosed.
I will scatter you postcards,

I will keep guard at Porta Ovila
where love-in-a-mist and thistle grow together.

I am the child who wept at the gate.
You are the land that dries the sea.

19.

This is riverless Siena.
I will not pay the ferryman with tears.

I will not let grief fill this void.
I will not speak in words of watered silk.

I will write how you refused
to sip from my water bottle despite your thirst.

I will not write of regret
such empty words clatter as a spoon in an empty bowl.

I am empty.
I will don my collarless shirt, wring the neck

of the last bottle, leave for Riga
Antananarivo, Astana, Bujumbura, Mbabana...

I will not find you pleached with stars
but, perhaps, tilting against the light, I may see you

where the sun catches on rock
where a drape of rain obscures the hills.

Translated into six languages, RUTH O'CALLAGHAN is an international poet who has read/lead workshops in Europe, Asia and the USA – where she was the only poet reading to nearly a thousand whilst the next day the audience was outnumbered by buffalo. A poet needs a sense of humour. A Hawthornden Fellow, international competition adjudicator, interviewer, reviewer, editor and mentor she works with both novice – aiming for that all important first collection – and more established poets. She has nine full collections and her book of interviews with 23 internationally eminent women poets is "a very important contribution to world literary history." (Professor Brant, Professor of Literature at King's College, London). She was awarded a gold medal at the XXX World Congress of Poets in Taiwan whilst her collaboration with women poets in Mongolia produced a fascinating book. She hosts two poetry venues in London which supports three Cold Weather Shelters and is also the poet for Strandlines, a multi-disciplinary project administered by Kings College, London.

www.salmonpoetry.com

*"Like the sea-run Steelhead salmon that thrashes upstream to its spawning ground,
then instead of dying, returns to the sea – Salmon Poetry Press
brings precious cargo to both Ireland and America in the poetry it publishes,
then carries that select work to its readership against incalculable odds."*

TESS GALLAGHER